3.00

D1561811

THE SCOTTISH RECORD SOCIETY
NEW SERIES
VOLUME 38

THE CLAN SHAW OF ARGYLL AND THE ISLES MACGILLECHAINNICH OF DALRIADA

THE SCOTTISH RECORD SOCIETY

Since its foundation in 1897 the Scottish Record Society has published numerous volumes of calendars and indices of public records and private muniments relating to Scotland. A list of the Society's publications and membership forms are available on request from the Honorary Secretary or online at www.scottishrecordsociety.org.uk.

Membership of the Society is open to all persons and institutions interested in its work.

The Armorial Bearings of Duncan Shaw of Chapelverna

THE CLAN SHAW OF ARGYLL AND THE ISLES MACGILLECHAINNICH OF DALRIADA

by
Duncan Shaw of Chapelverna
Representer of the Clan

EDINBURGH
2015

British Library Cataloguing-in Publication Data:
A catalogue record for this book is available from the
British Library

ISSN 01439448
ISBN 978-0-902054-52-3

Typeset by Victoria Arrowsmith-Brown
Printed by 4word Ltd, Page & Print Production

In memory of
Neil Shaw, younger of Chapelverna
1958-2013

CONTENTS

Preface

My research into the history of the Celtic Clan MacGilleChainnich of Dalriada, Shaw of Argyll and the Isles, from its early beginnings in Ireland and subsequent settlement in Argyll and the Isles, began many years after I had been invited by Charles John Shaw of Tordarroch to become a member of the Highland Clan of Shaw of which he had been recognized as Chief by the Lord Lyon King of Arms in 1970. I declined, being well aware that there were other Shaw family groups in various parts of Scotland unrelated to his Clan, one to which I belonged. Decades later, I commenced my researches and subsequently published an article in 2003.[1]

The systematic investigation into the history of the Clan has been founded solely on documentary evidence, in contradistinction to the frequent vague information in many family histories quoting tradition, taken at its face value, which is often misleading, unsubstantiated, and proving false. One particular difficulty has been the paucity of early documentary data, especially in the case of the lack of early unrecorded occupation of land, prior to the introduction of the feudal system.

Although deeply saddened on discovering the tragic final fate of the Clan in 1614, I am, nevertheless, gratified, beyond all expectation, at the eventual unfolding of the long significant history of my Clan from

---

[1] The Recovery of the Clan MacGilleChainnich of Dalriada. A Personal Pilgrimage, *The Scottish Genealogist,* Edinburgh, 2003, vol. L, 99-105.

its settling in Ireland on the remote edge of the then known world, its place in Argyll and Isles and the subsequent assumption of its English name.

After the Clan was broken and scattered four centuries ago, its history suddenly ended. On account of the ignorance of the Clan's Gaelic name, its Irish origins, and its important historic place within the Lordship of the Isles, its existence was forgotten. The Clan with its Gaelic surname was eventually correctly identified and, subsequently, recorded in the Lyon Office.

The tartan worn by members of the Clan is the Ancient Tartan of Macdonald of Sleat as descendants of followers of the Lord of the Isles.

I wish to express my appreciation to Sir Malcolm Innes of Edingight, then Lord Lyon King of Arms, for his continual encouragement, counsel and advice from the commencement of my research which has led finally to the restoration of the Clan and my appointment as Represener of the Clan in succession to the last Chief.

Primarily a historian of the sixteenth century, I acknowledge the debt owed to academic friends, particularly the late Dr John Bannerman for the earlier period, while footnotes reflect the important work of many other scholars who have lightened my task.

Duncan Shaw of Chapelverna,
Edinburgh,
27th January, 2015

Abbreviations

A.P.S. – *The Acts of the Parliaments of Scotland*, edd. Thomas Thomson and Cosmo Innes, Edinburgh, 1814-75, 12 vols.

Bannerman, *Dalriada* – *Studies in the History of Dalriada*, by John Bannerman, Edinburgh, 1974.

Budge, *Jura* – Donald Budge, *Jura, an Island of Argyll*, Glasgow, 1960.

C.S.S.R. 1418-1422 – *Calendar of Scottish Supplications to Rome 1418-1422*, edd. Rev. and Hon. E. R. Lindsay, and A. I. Cameron, Edinburgh, 1934.

C.S.S.R. 1423-1428 – *Calendar of Scottish Supplications to Rome 1423-1428*, ed. Annie I. Dunlop, Edinburgh, 1956.

C.S.S.R. 1428-1432 – *Calendar of Scottish Supplications to Rome, 1428-1432*, edd. Annie I. Dunlop and Ian B. Cowan, Edinburgh, 1970.

C.S.S.R. 1433-1447 – *Calendar of Scottish Supplications to Rome*, 1433-1447, edd. Annie I. Dunlop and David MacLauchlan, Glasgow, 1983.

C.S.S.R. 1447-1471 – *Calendar of Scottish Supplications to Rome*, *1447-1471*, edd. James Kirk, Roland J. Tanner and Annie I. Dunlop, Glasgow, 1996.

Cameron, *Justiciary Records of Argyll and the Isles 1664-1742* – *The Justiciary Records of Argyll and the Isles, 1664-1742*, ed. John Cameron, Edinburgh, 1949.

Campbell, *History of Craignish* – Herbert Campbell, The Manuscript History of Craignish, by Alexander Campbell, in *Miscellany of the Scottish History Society*, Edinburgh, 1926, iv., 175-296.

Collectanea - *Collectanea De Rebus Albanicis*, edd. W. F. Skene and D. Gregory, Iona Club, Edinburgh, 1847.

E.R. – *Exchequer Rolls of Scotland, 1264-1600*, edd. J. Stuart, i. and i-xiv. by G. Burnett, Edinburgh, 1878-1908.

List – List of Inhabitants in Strachur, 1693. Archives of Scotland, S.R.O.E.69/3/1 pp. 3-4.

MacPhail, *Strachur Writs* – Writs of and relating to the Campbells of Strachur, *Highland Papers*, ed. J. R. N. MacPhail, Edinburgh, 1934, vol. iv., pp. 1-55.

MacPhail, *Vatican Transcripts* – *Highland Papers*, ibid., pp. 131-188.

O.P.S. – *Origines parochiales Scotiae*, edd. Cosmo Innes, J. B. Brichan and others, 2 vols. in 3. Edinburgh, 1850-5.

Youngson, *Jura* – Peter Youngson, *Jura Island of Deer*, Edinburgh, 2001.

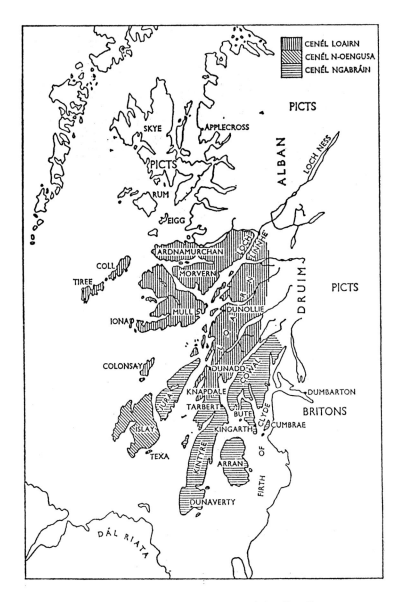

Geographical distribution of the Cenéla
©*John Bannerman, Studies in the History of Dalriada*

CHAPTER ONE

The Gaelic Name of the Clan Macgillechainnich of Dalriada, Shaw of Argyll and the Isles

On the emigration of the Celts to Ireland, some eventually settled in northern Ireland, long before their assumption of the Christian surname MacGille-Chainnich, son of the servant of Chainnich, in the sixth century, on conversion from druidism by St Chainnich: St Kenneth. However, most Clansmen usually continued to receive Celtic forenames, e.g., Angus, Donald, Duncan, Neil, etc. Such names are still rarer today among non Celtic Shaw families from other parts of Scotland.

The ancient MacGilleChainnichs migrated, with other Celtic Clans, from northern Ireland to Argyll and the Isles, living in the two regions of the Cenél nGabráin, Jura and Cowal. Many remained in Ireland, where variations of the name could be found in Ulster until the middle of the nineteenth century, while throughout Ireland the surname McIlhinney or other different versions of the original name are still current. No attempt has been made to include an account of the Irish Clan.

In Argyll and the Isles, the surname Shaw gradually replaced MacGilleChainnich when English became the sole official usage, in accord with the Statutes of Iona, of 1609, which stated, 'that the vulgar Inglishe toung be universalie plantit, and the Irishe language, which is

1

one of the cheif and principall causis of the continewance of barbaritie and uncivilitie amongis the inhabitantis of the Ilis and Heylandis, may be abolisheit and removit.'[1] All official documentation was thus recorded in English and gradually it became a linguistic necessity for those seeking employment, particularly when faced with incoming landowners, and the considerable Gaelic clearance from the Highlands and Islands.

As a consequence, the accurate Gaelic surname and it origins were forgotten. The first confusing statement regarding the name of the Clan, which led subsequent writers astray, appeared in 1926. The Reverend Hector Cameron, minister of Oban, maintained 'that the word Schaw was adopted as a surname by the McGillechaynichs from the Ayrshire surname being not altogether unlike the name by which they had been known in Gaelic viz., Sitheachair, or rather Mac-Shitheachair – their ancestors have been 'wolfers' (wolfkillers) to the MacDonalds.' He states that 'Mac-Shitheach(air) became MacSheathaich, MacSheatha-naich and so MacIllesheathanaich, which thus accounts for the Clan name.[2] However, it was explicitly shown to be erroneous in 1934 by J. R. N. Macphail in 'Campbell of Strachur Writs' who noted that the Gaelic surname meant the son of the servant of St Chainnich or Kenneth.[3]

---

[1] *Register of the Privy Council of Scotland*, ed. David Masson, Edinburgh, 1891, x. 671-2.

[2] Campbell, *History of Craignish*, 280n.

[3] MacPhail, *Strachur Writs*, 48n.

This was overlooked and G. F. Black, *The Surnames of Scotland*, New York, 1946, states, 'The name Shaw means 'son of the wolf' from 'sitheach' (Middle Irish 'sidhech'), an old Gaelic name for the animal.' This was repeated in 1960[4] by Donald Budge and again, in 2001, when the incorrect spelling of the name, as noted in the foregoing statement by Cameron, is repeated by Youngson.[5] However, it should be noted that even Neil Shaw, for many years secretary to An Comunn Gaidhealach, spelt his Gaelic surname as Macillesheathanaich: he died in 1961.[6]

This interpretation of the name is still continually reiterated, appearing in two publications during the year of the Gathering of the Clans in Edinburgh, 2009.[7]

Thus, as Samuel Johnson stated, 'Languages are the pedigree of nations' and so the pedigree of the Clan was gone. In addition, generations of Gaelic speakers in Argyll and the Isles were unaware of the undermining of their language. Thus, as in Tacitus, 'The language of the conqueror in the mouth of the conquered is ever the language of the slave.'

The replacing of the Clan's Gaelic surname by Shaw was not unique and many double surnames appear in the records of registers of births and marriages. In

---

[4] Budge, *Jura*, 168-9.
[5] Youngson, *Jura*, 512-4.
[6] Budge, *Jura*, 169.
[7] John Abernethy, *Collins Scottish Names*, Glasgow, 52, issued free with the *Scotsman* newspaper, and *Scottish Names*, anonymous, Waverley Books, New Lanark, 267-8, which was remaindered within months.

by Alison Cathcart.[14] A background account of the manifold tragedies has been given by Michael Hechter.[15]

---

[14] Alison Cathcart, *Kinship and Clientage: Highland Clanship, 1451-1609*, Leiden, 2006.

[15] Michael Hechter, *Internal Colonialism. The Celtic Fringe in British National Development, 1536-1966*, London, 1975.

CHAPTER 2

The Origin of the Clan in Ireland and its Arrival in Argyll and the Isles

The Celts and their civilisation originated many centuries ago in central Europe and Spain before some of the tribes settled in Ireland and, subsequently, in Dalriada which were often small units living in sparsely populated areas. While statistics cannot be accurately determined, it has been estimated that the population of Roman Britain was between half a million[1] and one and a half million,[2] whereas, in Scotland, in 1300, it has been estimated that the population was about 400,000.[3] This has to be taken into account when considering the size of Clans throughout the period, which would appear, at times, to be exaggerated.

The legend of the settlement of Ireland from the Flood to the pre-Christian period is enshrined in the story of Tuan, son of Cairill. This narrates that he arrived after the Flood and witnessed subsequent history, assuming four forms, one of which was an eagle. He claimed that he had been reborn as the son of king Carell and, in his old age, recounted his personal history to St Finnian. The eagle on the shield and the crest of

---

[1] R. G. Collingwood, 'Town and Country in Roman Britain', in *Antiquary*, iii., 1929, 262-76.

[2] H. Randall, 'Population and Agriculture in Roman Britain', in *Antiquary*, iv., 1930, 80-90.

[3] Rt. Hon. Lord Cooper, *Supra Crepidam,* Edinburgh, 1951, 14.

the Representer of the Clan is a reminder of the Clan's pre-Christian origins.

The Clan MacGilleChainnich, i.e., the son of the servant of Chainnich – St Kenneth – had its beginning in Glasnevin as recorded in the Life of St Columba[4] when Columba visited the founder St Mobhi and the others. It is recorded that there were fifty studying there together with Chainnech, Comgall and Cairan, whose booths were to the west of the water.

It is most probable that there had previously been a community of druids there. Giraldus Cambrensis maintained, for example, that Brigit built a community on the site of a previous female druid centre.[5]

Irish Celtic Christian teaching mirrored that of the druids. Camille Jullian narrates that the druids 'gathered round them members of Gallic families and taught them all that they knew or believed concerning the world, the human soul, and the gods. A few of these scholars stayed with their masters until they had reached the age of twenty years but it is clear that those who were to become priests received the lion's share of attention'.[6] It is recorded in the Ulster Cycle, that Cathbad, chief druid at the court of Conchobar, king of Ulster, was overwhelmed by the number of youths who were desirous of learning his art.

---

[4] 'The Life of St Columba from the Edinburgh MS', in *Scottish Gaelic Studies,* Edinburgh, 1928. ii. 131.

[5] P. B. Ellis, *A Brief History of the Druids,* London, 2002, 158.

[6] C. Jullian, *Recherches sur la religion gauloise,* Bordeaux, 1903, 157.

The MacGilleChainnich Clan were of the Cenél nEóghain group, a collective clan name for tribes descended from Eoghain, son of Neall of the Nine Hostages, the fifth century High King of Ireland: they were of the priestly order[7] and chiefly located in Derry, Tyrone and Donegal. On arrival in Scotland they settled in Jura and Cowal, the areas occupied by the Cenél nGabráin,[8] as is evident from the distribution of the surname within Jura and Cowal. The other two Clans of Cenél nGabráin, who also lived in Cowal, were the Lamonts and the MacEwens.

As with the druids, some of the followers of Chainnich would have been in his company when he visited Iona soon after the arrival of Columba in 565. Adamnan tells that he was received with honour and hospitality.

There is a burial ground – Kil-Chainnich – in Iona and several churches dedicated to him in Scotland.

---

[7] D. S. Thomson, 'Gaelic Learned Orders and Literari in Medieval Scotland', in *Scottish Studies*, Edinburgh, 1968. xii. 57-78.

[8] Bannerman, *Dalriada*, 116: cf. John Bannerman, 'The Dal Riata and Northern Ireland in the Sixth and Seven Centuries', in *Celtic Studies – Essays in Memory of Angus Matheson 1912-1962*, edd., James Carney and Robert Greene, London. 1968, 1-11, and Dauvit Brown, *The Irish Identity of the Kingdom of the Scots*, Woodbridge, 1999.

CHAPTER 3

Chapelverna

Within the area of Cowal, also another area of settlement by the Cenél nGabráin,[1] is to be found Chapelverna, a seat of the Clan MacGilleChainnich, which is of very ancient origin. There was once the remains of a stone circle at Clachan, Strachur, which was removed during the building of the schoolhouse.[2] This indicates the presence in Strachur of a druid community prior to its becoming Christian.[3] It was the site of a chapel dedicated to St Ernan, the uncle of St Columba of Iona and a contemporary of St Kenneth, who was one of the twelve who accompanied St Columba and Kenneth (Chainnich) from Derry in northern Ireland to Iona. St Ernan may indeed have visited there as he was abbot of a monastery, possibly on Jura. He is reputed to be buried at Keils in Jura, an ancient homeland of the Clan. Within Dalriada, he had roots in earliest Celtic Christianity and indicates a close connection between the Clan and the Iona saints. The name Chapelverna, recorded as 'Chapel' in William Roy's map, based on his Military Survey of Scotland, 1740 to 1755, is the ancient seat of 'Celtic barons of the

---

[1] Bannerman, *Dalriada*, 116.
[2] www.themodernantiquarian.com/site/12923/clachan _strachur_schoolhouse.
[3] *Adamnan's life of St Columba,* edd. A. O. and M. O. Anderson, Edinburgh, 1961, 306-7.

Clan'.[4] Later, the village assumed the regional name Strachur.

A family of the Clan lived in Chapelverna, a half merk land valued £1.7.9,[5] for generations prior to the demise of Muireadhaich I, earl of Menteith, in 1213, who had exercised a certain authority over Cowal and Kintyre,[6] when the lands of Strachur came into the possession of Duncan Campbell, son of Dugald Campbell, 14th of Lochawe, and younger brother of Gillespie, ancestor of the dukes of Argyll.[7] The family continued to live there. The earliest documentary evidence is the feu charter of 1580 granted by Colin Campbell of Strachur to Gillespie MacGilleChainnich. The charter was issued some years after the lands of Strachur were confirmed to him by Mary, Queen of Scots, during a visit she paid there. It stated that the MacGilleChainnich family had 'lived there beyond the memory of man'.[8]

This indicated that the land had been held under the old Celtic tribal system: land held allodially – of God. The Clan land was divided between the cuntrie and the duthus.[9] The latter was territory apportioned to a

---

[4] MacPhail, *Strachur Writs,* 48n.

[5] The Cowal Valuation Records of 1721, Archibald Brown, *The History of Cowal,* Greenock, 1908, 26.

[6] *Red Book of Menteith,* ed. William Fraser, Edinburgh, 1880, vol. i. 41.

[7] *Burke's Landed Gentry of Great Britain,* London, 2011. 179.

[8] MacPhail, *op.cit.,* 47-48.

[9] Cynthia L. Neville, *Land Law and People in Medieval Scotland,* Edinburgh, 2012.

Chief, who granted parts of it at easy rents to members of the derbfine. Once a family had occupied the land for four generations it became theirs by right. This MacGilleChainnich family was described as 'Celtic barons'.[10]

Unlike the tragedies faced by the Clans Lamont and MacEwen, caused by the Campbells in Cowal, the MacGilleChainnichs remained there bearing their Gaelic name and enjoying neighbourly relations with the Campbells of Strachur until their departure in the early nineteenth century; this was possibly because the MacGilleChainnichs may have originally been priests and, as such, had been scholarly non combatants. The members of the family, so far traced, are:

Gillespie, 1580,[11]

Ian Roy, 1598 and 1617,[12]

Archibald McIan Roy, 1617, 1632,[13]

Ian McGillespie VcIan Roy, after 1632,[14]

John, 1678,[15]

John, 1751,[16]

John, 1770, who married Susanna, daughter of Archibald McGillespie of Balliemore, later of

---

[10] MacPhail, *op.cit.* 48n.

[11] Ibid., 47-9.

[12] Ibid., 43, 47-9.

[13] Ibid.

[14] Ibid.

[15] Cameron, *Justiciary Records of Argyll and the Isles, 1664-1742*, i., 97.

[16] The Cowal Valuation Records of 1721, *op.cit.*, 26.

Glansluan, minister of Strachur,[17] giving his residence as Chapel, although his holding was still recorded as Chapelverna.[18]
John 1822.[19]

The last Clan family left Chapelverna early in the nineteenth century, although the village continued to be known as Chapel. The arable part of the holding was later merged with Strachurmore, although the large remaining area skirting Strachur continued to be known as the Chapel field. Fortunately, a search of the sasine register contained one entry regarding Chapelverna and thus made it possible for the property to be delimited and recovered in January 2003. Two years later, the Clan was re-established on recognition by Robin Blair, the Lord Lyon King of Arms, of Duncan MacGilleChainnich of Dalriada, Shaw of Argyll and the Isles, in succession to the last Chief killed in 1614.

---

[17] *Fasti Ecclesiae Scoticanae*, ed. H. Scott, second edition, Edinburgh, 1923, iv. 45.
[18] *A Directory of Land Ownership in Scotland, c. 1770*, ed. L. R. Timperley, Scottish Record Society, Edinburgh, 1976, 44, 99.
[19] Deed of 1822 in the writer's possession.

CHAPTER 4

Finlaggan and Iona

On Iona there was originally a druid community which became the site of a Celtic monastery established by Columba who came from Ireland with others in 565, after having founded a monastery in Derry; he was later joined by Kenneth, i.e. Chainnich from Ireland, with followers, who became known as MacGilleChainnich. His name is given to a cemetery at the Abbey.

Venerated by the Scottish kings from earliest Celtic times, it was the burial place of early Scottish kings. In 1549, graves of forty-eight Scottish, eight Norwegian and four Irish kings were recorded. None is now identifiable as, by the end of the seventeenth century, the inscriptions were worn away.

St Columba and his followers built a small monastery from wood, wattle and daub. The monastery was sacked during Viking incursions over a considerable period. It survived and was subsequently established as an Abbey of the Order of St Benedict from northern Ireland in 1203.[1] The Pope, because of the distance of Norway from Iona, gave the abbot the use of the mitre and ring and other episcopal privileges,[2] simultaneously declaring that abbot and convent were not to be summoned to the

---

[1] *Annals of Ulster,* ed. W. M. Hennessy, Dublin, 1887-1901, ii., 230-2.

[2] A. O. Anderson, *Early Sources of Scottish History, A.D. 500-1286*, 1922, ii., 361n., 231.

chapter general of the Benedictines in Scotland.[3] This gave the abbot a singular status both in the Church and in the Council of the Lord of the Isles, of which he was an *ex officio* member. It should not be overlooked that the contact was later kept with England. The most significant cultural occurrence was when Donald, eighth Lord of the Isles, studied divinity at Oxford about 1378.[4]

The first member of the Clan found at Iona was Dominic MacGilleChainnich, a priest, the son of a priest of the Order of Benedict and an unmarried woman, which was not unusual at that time: a continuation of the Celtic tradition of non-celibate clergy. A mandate was given by Pope Benedict XIII, to Theodore Bloc, O.Crucit., bishop of Sodor and Man, with others, dated 22nd December, 1408, to permit him to become a monk in the Abbey and 'to assure him of a portion of the goods of the monastery' as 'a large part of the choir and the chapter and other buildings are in ruins and a great part of the lands of the monastery unlawfully occupied by wicked men'.[5]

On the death in 1421 of John MacAlister, the abbot, the convent unanimously elected Dominic as successor, under the patronage of Donald, Lord of the Isles, who

---

[3] *Calendar of Entries in the Papal Registers, Letters,* London. 1894, i., 231.

[4] *Rotuli Scotiae in Turri Londinensi et in domo capitulari Westmonasteriensi asservati,* edd. David Macpherson, John Caley, W. Illingworth, London, 1814-19, ii., 402.

[5] *Papal letters to Scotland of Benedict XIII of Avignon,* 1394-1419, ed. Francis McGurk, Edinburgh, 1976, 194.

had retired to the monastery prior to his death in 1423. This was in accord with the ancient Celtic tradition, 'and hath made us kings and priests unto God'.[6] 'Many Celtic princes underwent the clericatus, entering the monastery and leaving the throne to his heir.'[7] The abbot had a high constitutional status in relation to the royal succession.[8]

On 6th December, 1421, steps were taken at the Roman Curia and Neil Celestini, bachelor of both laws, rector of Kilchoman, vicar general of Richard, bishop of Sodor, brought apostolic letters from Rome. It was stated, 'At the petition of Dominicus, (containing some doubt of the validity of the election and consecration and hold that the monastery is still void), the Pope has now confirmed the same by apostolic authority'. However, it was stated 'As the monastery is not found taxed in the extant books of the Camera, the Roman Curia requires to have full notice of the rents, profits and value for the purpose of fixing the taxation due on account of apostolic promotion'.[9] The taxation was, subsequently, fixed and over the next few years duly

---

[6] Revelation, i., v. 6.

[7] W. F. Skene, *Celtic Scotland,* Edinburgh, 1889, sec. edition, i., 185f. and cf. A. Macquarrie, 'Kings, Lords and Abbots: power, patronage and the medieval monastery of Iona' in *Transactions of the Gaelic Society of Inverness, liv. 1984-6, 355-75.*

[8] *'Royal Succession and Abbatial Prerogative in Adamnan's Vita Columba'* in *Peritia,* Turnhout, 1985, vi., 83-103.

[9] Annie I. Cameron, *The Apostolic Camera and Scottish Benefices 1418-1488,* Oxford, 1934, 3.

paid.[10] This was followed by confirmation and consecration by Richard Payk, bishop of Sodor, and blessed by him. It is recorded that the monastery was still destroyed in its buildings and rents by continuous wars.[11] With the Avignon papacy having ended in 1419, Dominic petitioned Martin V for papal confirmation and received a mandate of provision by apostolic authority. He was immediately faced with domestic administrative responsibilities as Neil Celestini, rector of Kilchoman, vicar general in spirituals of Richard Payk, bishop of Sodor, was mandate of chamberlain of the College and chamberlain depute of Camera, Rome, with powers of citing, upon oath, of taking depositions and compulsion by ecclesiastical censure and other remedies of law. Before Celestini delivered the apostolic letters to the abbot, he was instructed to make inquisition anent all and sundry the fruits, rents, profits and dues of the said monastery. This had to be sent to the Camera within a year, so that the taxation of the monastery was fixed so that the rights of the Camera, College and familiars were not neglected.[12]

Dominic probably had an association with Donald, Lord of the Isles, prior to the death of his father who was responsible for the introduction of the Benedictines to Iona and whose successors continued as patrons of the Abbey.[13] The more significant event was the concern by James I with the state of the monasteries and, at the

---

[10] Ibid., 6, 9, 10.
[11] *C.S.S.R., 1418-1422*, 264-5.
[12] Summarised from Annie I. Cameron, *op.cit.*, 3.
[13] *C.S.S.R., 1447-1471*, 1201.

62. Scottis-men suld bring na man furth of Ireland, without an Testimonial.

It is seene speedful, that gif onie Schip-man of Scotland passis with letters of the Kingis Depute, in *Ireland*, that he receive na man into his Schip to bring with him to the Realme of *Scotland*, bot gif that man have ane letter or certaintie of the Lord of that land, qhhair he shippis, for quhat cause he ccummis in this Realme.

63. Anent Ireland men command in Scottis Schippis.

That quhen he commis in onie Haven of *Scotland*, that he ryde on anker, and hald within shipbuird all men that he bringis with them, quhill he send for the Kingis Bailie, or a Depute of the Towne of the Haven, that he cummis in, that the men may be examined and see of the Kingis behalfe their persones, and quhat charge they have be letter of uther way, quhidder it be profite or predudice to the King, or the Kinrik (kingdom): And gif onie prejudice of the deed be founded, they sall be arreisted, and presented to the Schireffis person, quhill the King have done his will on them.

The close connections from Scotland to northern Ireland continued. However, these enactments had a more significant restriction for non-clerical members of the Clan who travelled to northern Ireland for non-ecclesiastical affairs and were supporters of the Lord of the Isles in his continuing to strive to maintain his influence there.

As a member of the Council of the Lordship of the Isles, convening at Finlaggan, Islay, the abbot's role in its government was significant, particularly as he served the successive Lords of the Isles and became closely associated with them. Thomas Barry, bishop of Ossory, received a papal mandate 'to enquire into certain matters relating to the Monastery of St Columba, *in non*, with powers. 8th January, 1444'.[17]

He was faced with civil strife towards the end of his life and participated in the discussions within the Council of the Isles. Duncan MacGilleChainnich, undoubtedly a relative, was secretary to John, earl of Ross, and Lord of the Isles, before 14th June, 1456,[18] at Finlaggan. He was later appointed locally archdeacon of the Isles[19] when he accompanied Ronald of the Isles, as ambassadors to Edward IV, king of England. The Lord of the Isles promised to ratify and abide by agreements made by them, at Ardtornich, 19th October, 1461. The two were at Westminster on 8th and 13th February, 1462.[20] Dominic remained in his Abbey and served the council of the Isles, unlike George Lauder, bishop of Argyll, who petitioned the Roman Curia that, 'on account of strife raging between temporal lords and other magnates of his diocese, and the tumults of wars and dangers arising therefrom, is unable to reside safely and befittingly in the diocese of Argyll and

---

[17] J. R. N. MacPhail, History of the Macdonalds, in *Highland Papers*, vol. i., Edinburgh, 1914, 82-92.

[18] *Acts of the Lords of the Isles, 1336-1493*, edd. Jean Munro and R. W. Munro, Edinburgh, 1986, 92.

[19] *Fasti Ecclesiae Scoticanae Medii Aevi Ad Annum 1638*, edd. D. R. Watt and A. L. Murray, Scottish Record Society, Edinburgh, 2003, 273.

[20] *Rotuli Scotiae,* op.cit., ii.

exercise his jurisdiction'.[21] He died after 1467:[22] a decade prior to the fall of the Lordship.

Surviving, in pride of place within the Abbey, is his full length carved stone effigy.[23] The inscription was readable in c.1695 by Martin Martin[24] and in 1772 by Thomas Pennant.[25] It is 1.98m long by 0.57m wide, carved from Carsaig sandstone: the same stone as was used for the restoration of the Abbey. It is worn and lacks the base-slab, originally supported on four carved pedestals. The abbot is dressed in full eucharistic vestments and carrying a crozier. His head rests on a tasselled double pillow supported by two angels and, at the feet, two crouching lions.

The previous years had been troubled times and continued to be so. In April, 1462, George Lauder, bishop of Argyll, appealed to the Pope for leave of absence.[26] He may have left his diocese before then as he attended parliament in Edinburgh in March, 1461.[27] As he had not received a reply, he sought an answer in July the following year.[28] There is no record of his death

[21] *C.S.S.R., 1447-1471,* 903.

[22] *Fasti,* op cit., 36.

[23] *The Royal Commission on the Ancient and Historical Monuments of Scotland, Argyll, An Inventory of the Monuments of Scotland,* Edinburgh, *1982,* vol. iv., Iona, 231.

[24] Martin Martin, *Description of the Western Islands of Scotland,* Stirling, 1934, 287.

[25] Thomas Pennant, *A Tour of Scotland and Voyage to the Highlands,* London, 1772, i., 253.

[26] *C.S.S.R.,* 1447-1471, 903.

[27] *A.P.S.,* xii., 28.

[28] *C.S.S.R.,* 1447-1471, 953.

and his successor, Robert Colquhoun,[29] was not provided until 24th April, 1475, and died before 14th February, 1496[30] after the fall of the Lordship of the Isles.

On the death of Dominic, the organisation and status of the Abbey deteriorated as the power of the patron, John, Lord of the Isles, decreased at home and with Colin Campbell, lord of Glenorchy, the ambassador of James III at the Papal Curia from 1466.[31] This culminated in the failure of Angus, son of Angus of the Isles, to be granted provision, although having been postulated as abbot of the Abbey on Dominic's death in 1465.[32] However, on the death of Dominic MacGilleChainnich, his successor was John MacKinnon, from 1467 to his death in 1498. After the fall of the Lordship of the Isles, Archibald, second earl of Argyll, became the patron of the Abbey and petitioned the Pope to make the Abbey into the cathedral of the diocese of the Isles,[33] but the change was not made and John Campbell was appointed commendator of the abbacy on 1st April, 1499.[34] The last commendator, Alexander Campbell, continued in office until the abbacy was annexed to the bishopric of the Isles in 1615.

---

[29] C. Eubel, *Hierarchia Catholica Medii Aevi,* sec. edition, Munster, 1914, ii., 179.

[30] John Dowden, *The Bishops of Scotland*, Glasgow, 1912, 387.

[31] *C.S.S.R.,* 1447-1471, 1095, 1099, 1106, 1109, 1116.

[32] Ibid., 1018.

[33] *The Register of the Privy Seal of Scotland,* i.1488-1529, ed. M. Livingstone, Edinburgh, 1908, 184.

[34] MacPhail, *Vatican Transcripts*, 185-8.

The first recorded Clan member, after the abbot, is Meritii MacGilleChainnich, rector of the parish of St Congar of Knoydart, who held the benefice for eight years prior to 1427,[35] the patron being the Lord of the Isles.[36]

Other three persons occur in the papal registers and are, undoubtedly, the sons and daughter of Dominic: Dominicus Dominici, O.S.B., who petitioned the Roman Curia, shortly after his father had been appointed abbot, to hold two benefices in view of the Abbey's poverty. He was for a time rector of St Conan in Waternish, also known as Kilchoman in Skye.[37] He died in 1428.[38] There was one member of the family, illustrating the close connection with Donald, Lord of the Isles, who personally supplicated the Pope on behalf of Adam Dominici, son of a member of the Order of St Benedict,[39] vicar of Kilvechaon, in 1427,[40] supported by Angus of the Isles, bishop of the Isles, brother of Alexander, Lord of the Isles, where the parsonage teinds had been annexed to Iona since at least 1421.[41] Cristina Dominici, daughter of the same, was a canoness of the Augustinian nunnery of Iona, founded

---

[35] *C.S.S.R.,* 1423-1428, 180-1.

[36] *O.P.S.,* ii., 204-5.

[37] *C.S.S.R.,* 1418-1422, 265, 267, 275, ibid., ii., 180, 203-4, 206.

[38] *C.S.S.R.,* 1423-1428, 203-4, 206.

[39] Ibid., 182.

[40] *C.S.S.R.,* 1418-1422, 269, 275, ibid., 1423-1428, 182, 184.

[41] Ian B. Cowan, *The Parishes of Medieval Scotland,* Scottish Record Society, Edinburgh, 100, 109.

by Beathag, sister of Reginald, son of Somerled, and received papal dispensations for defect of birth, in 1422[42] and in 1428,[43] indicating her hope of promotion in the order, but nothing further is known. She may have become the prioress.

---

[42] MacPhail, *Vatican Transcripts*, 175-6, and *C.S.S.R., 1418-1422*, i., 279-80.

[43] *C.S.S.R.*, 1423-1428, 183-4.

CHAPTER 5

Jura until the Breaking of the Clan

Jura, as with Cowal, was the home of the Clan from its arrival from Ireland, but was ruled by Norway from 1098 until 1266 on the signing of the Treaty of Perth. Thus, on account of the paucity of records concerning Jura, no account can be given of the Clan MacGilleChainnich in Jura until after the fall of the Lord of the Isles. This had an immediate effect on the Clan there and led to the gradual breakdown of the co-ordinated organisation of the Clan and the loss of secure residence of its members.

In the spring of 1563, the MacGregors were in Ireland pursued by Archibald Campbell, fifth earl of Argyll, and John Stewart, fourth earl of Atholl, who were commissioned to apprehend them. They returned in the autumn 'and have sued the queen to be received in mercy.' James MacDonald of Dunnyveg interceded for them as revealed in a letter of 24th October, 1564, to Thomas Randolph and William Cecil.[1] The MacGregors would seem to have gone there where the MacGilleChainnichs, although broken like those in Scotland, were allies of Shane O'Neill and therefore in contact with James MacDonald of Dunnyveg. On one occasion, in June of that year, Fardarroch MacGilleChainnich, jointly with O'Neill and 300 or 400

---

[1] *Calendar of State Papers relating to Scotland and Mary Queen of Scots, 1547-1603*, ed. J. Bain, Edinburgh, 1898, ii. 89.

men, had captured a ship belonging to a Wigtown merchant driven ashore at Carlingford which they looted and destroyed.[2] During the following year, O'Neil and Fardarroch MacGilleChainnich were involved in further piracy in Ireland.[3]

This is the last recorded incident connecting the Clan with events in Ireland.

The first Scottish incident in the disorder facing the MacGilleChainnichs, with the fall of the lordship of the Isles, is revealed in connection with the actions of the Clan MacGregor, as shown in the decision of the Privy Council of 22nd September, 1563.[4] This is clear from a letter from Colin Campbell of Glenorchy to Archibald Campbell, fifth earl of Argyll, of 6th July, 1565, which refers to Gregor Roy MacGregor's knowing the whereabouts of two MacGilleChainnichs, bonded servants of John Stewart, fourth earl of Atholl, whom Gregor promised to surrender to Atholl.[5] In the following month, Atholl was appointed Lieutenant of the north with wide jurisdiction. Subsequently, Colin Campbell of Glenorchy wrote to the earl of Argyll, on 20th August, 1570, that 'had your lordship caused [Colin Campbell] the laird of Otter to have delivered the Kottar Dowe and also [Colin Campbell,] the laird of

---

[2] Ibid., ii. 64.

[3] Ibid.

[4] *The Register of the Privy Council of Scotland,* 1545-1568, ed. J. H. Burton, Edinburgh, 1877, i. 248f.

[5] *Campbell Letters, 1559-1583,* ed. J. E. A. Dawson, Edinburgh, 1997. 102-3, cf. M. MacGregor, A Political History of the MacGregors before 1571, Edinburgh, Ph.D. Thesis, 1989, 350-1.

Ardkinglas friends to have delivered Mac-GilleChainnich and as many as that house had under them that took part with the Clan Gregor, their troubles would not have come upon me lately.'[6] Gregor MacGregor, constable of Kilchurn castle, at the north of Loch Awe, in a letter to Colin Campbell of Glenorchy, mentioned some of the Clan Mac-GilleChainnich as being in the area, where they seem to have been a distinct family cattle owning group.[7]

The Clan's broken state was further seriously confronted by the Scottish Parliament passing an Act on 8th July, 1587, *'For the Quieting and Keeping in Obedience of the Disordered Subjects, Inhabitants of the Borders, Highlands and Islands.'*

This enacted, 'That all landlords and bailies of the land on the borders and in the highlands where broken men have dwelt or presently dwell, contained in a roll inserted in the end of this present act, shall be charged to find sufficient caution and surety, landed men in the in-country to the contentment of our sovereign lord and his privy council between now and 1st October, 1587, or within 15 days after the charge upon conditions following, under the pain of rebellion, and, if they fail, the said day being past, to put them to the horn: that is to say, if any of their men, tenants, servants and indwellers upon their lands, rooms, steadings and possessions or within their bailiaries commit any masterful reiving, theft, or reset of theft, depredations open and avowed, fire-raising upon deadly feuds

---

[6] Ibid., 180.
[7] Ibid., 194-5.

protected and maintained by their masters, that the landlords and bailies upon whose lands and in whose jurisdiction they dwell shall bring and present the persons complained upon before [Archibald Campbell, seventh earl of Argyll]. Our sovereign lord's justice or his deputes.'

Appended to the Act was 'the roll of the names of the landlords and bailies of lands dwelling on the borders and in the highlands where broken men have dwelt and presently dwell.'

The appended roll of names of the landlords and bailies of lands dwelling in the borders where broken men have dwelt and presently dwell numbered 24, of those in the highlands and islands 105 and of Clans that have captains, chiefs and chieftains on whom they depend 54.

Action against Angus MacDonald of Dunnyveg was re-enforced when parliament, in April, 1593, summoned him and his accomplices for treason.[8]

Shortly thereafter, James VI sent instructions to Robert Melville of Murdocairnie, the Scottish ambassador to queen Elizabeth, on 4th June, 1593, indicating his intention of taking action against MacDonald and his followers, both in Scotland and Ireland, stating:

'Beside these occasions necessarily craving the supply of forces, there is yet another most requisite, for which we must crave the aid of our dearest sister, of a ship or two with munitions and powder for the expugnation of certain houses in the Western Isles of

---

[8] *A.P.S.*, iv. 4-5

follow and obey him and his heirs whatsoever place he and his aforesaid transport themselves in the country or without; and shall obey them as native men ought and should do to their Chief in time coming. For which the said Ronald for himself and his heirs, binds and obliges himself and them to be a good chief and master to the said persons and their succession as his native men and to give them their duty that they and their succession of men and women ought to have after *calps con torm* to the use of the country and this to stand as a perpetual deposition, forever. Upon which the said Ronald took instruments in the hands of me, notary underwritten, day, year and place aforesaid before these witnesses.'[13]

Bonds of maintenance and manrent themselves were not thought of as being primarily legally binding documents; the sanctions on those who made them were social rather than legal.[14] Even when attempts were made to submit a bond of manrent with other documentation, supporting evidence in a case before a justifier's court in mid fifteenth century, the case dragged on for five years without resolution.[15]

A further four were subscribed, with others, from 1612 to 1621.[16] Thus, the original native population,

---

[13] Ibid., 198.

[14] Wormald, *op.cit.*, 131.

[15] H. L. MacQueen, 'The Kin of Kennedy, 'Kenkynnol' and the Common Law' in *Medieval Scotland, Crown, Lordship and Community*, edd. A. Grant and K. J. Stringer, Edinburgh, 1993.

[16] Wormald, *op.cit.*, 251-52.

many landless, was in bonded service. This action was taken in spite of such bonds being outlawed by Act of Parliament, chapter 17, 20th June, 1555. No action would have been taken against Ronald Campbell as his kinsman, Archibald Campbell, seventh earl of Argyll, was Justice General of Scotland.

Pressure continued to be exerted on the MacGillechainnichs and a further and much more detailed bond of manrent was secured by Barrichbeyan in 1604:

At the Ile of Ellanan in Kreggenis, the xxj day of Februer in the zeir of God 1604.

It is appointit, contractit finallie endit and aggreit between the pairteis underwrittin.

To Wit:

Rannald Campbell of Barrachybyen, with consent and
    assent of his germane brethir,
Alexr. George, and
Archd. Campbellis and
Ewir Macgillespik vek ewir bane of Lergachony, and
    certane utheris, thair kin and freindis on the ane
    pairt, and
Donald makangus vekgillichaynich,
Duncan oig,
Neill,
Gilliecreist,
Gillecallum,
John ower,
John oig, his germane brethir,
And siklike
Johne makdonill vekconchie vekillehaynych,

Duncan oig, his germane brothir,
Donald makeane vekdonill vekillehaynych,
Angus oig and
Johne Dow, his brethir,
Donald oig makdonill vekdowsey vekgillehaynych,
Gillecallum, his sone, and
Duncane oig, his broder sone, on the uther pairt.
 In maner, forme and eftir followis:

 That is to say. Forsamekle as Johne dow Campbell,
broder germane to the said Rannnald, wes slane in the
Ile of Jewar be Angus Makdonill of Dwnyvaigis
schaweis in the moneth of July the zeir of God 1602 and
siklike it was notourlie knawin and kend that John
makdonilll vegillechreist vekgillechaynych and Neill
makane vek donill vekgillechaynych wes art and part of
the slachter of the sd. umqle. Johne dow Campbell in
putting handis in his body, halding him in handis and
taking his wappynis fra him and striking (him) thro' the
body with his sword and siklike, manifestlie knawin
and kend that Angus Macdonchie vekgillehaynych and
Neill makdonill vekdonchie vek gillehaynych wer art
and part of the said slachter in sa far as thay kepit
sacretie fallowschip and company oft and syndrie tymes
eftir the said slachter with the personis, takeris and
slayeris of the said John dow, thay and the committaris
of the said slachter being then schaweis to the said
Angus makdonill of Dwnivaig and committing in the
menetyme Raif and spulze within the erll of ergylis
cuntrie throw the quhilks it chancit the said Rannald
Campbell and his compliers to slay the said Angus
makdonchy Vegillehaynych father of the said Donald

makangus and his said brethir and siclike to slay the said Neill makdonill vekdonchie broder sone to the said umqle, Angus.

Nevirtheles baith the said pairteis for sindrie causes moving thame and in speciall becaus the said Donald makangus and his brethir germane foresaid ar sister sones to the said Rannald; and baith the said pairteis thinkis (it) mair necessar and kyndlie and commodious for baith thair weilfare that familiaritie, friendschip, kyndness, and gude nychtnourheid be observit and kepitt amangis thame in tymes coming (and) nocht innimitie and fellony.

Thairfoir howevir the saidis slachteris on ather syd hes proceidit and bene comittit baith the saidis pairteis has remittit and forgevin and be the tenor of thir presentis fullelie remittis and forgevis ilk ane of thame uther of the saidis slachteris comittit on ather syde and the rancour and malice of thair hertis conceavit aganis utheris thairrthrow.

That is to say, the said Rannald Campbell for hymselff and brethren foirsaid, kyn and freindis and assistaris Remittis the forenamit Clan makille-haynych, thair airis and successouris, for evir, the slachter of the said Johne dow his broder and all that may be imput to thame thairthrow in the law or by the law. And in lykmaner the foresaid Clan makillechaynich for thameselffis, thair barnis and successouris kyn freindis and assistaris Remittis the foirnameit Rannald Campbell his airis, brethir and compliers being art and paiart of the slachter of the said Angus and Neill, and all that may be input to thame and ilk ane of thame thairthrow in the law and by the law;

And baith the saidis pairteis bindis and oblissis thame their airis and successouris to be leill trew and of auld freindis to uther in all tymes cuming and to fortefie maintene and assist ilk ane of thame utheris in all their lesum actionis caussis and querrellis aganis all maner of man except the Erllis of Argyle thair successouris and surename being exceptit by the said Ranald and his foirsaidis and Makalne of Doward and his successouris, being exceptit be the said Clan Makillehaynych. And quhilk of the saidis pairteis failzeis in fulfilling thair part of this present Contract but violatis the samin Bindis and oblissis thame thair airis executouris and assigneis to content and pay the sowm of ane thowsand merkis, gude and usuall monie of Scotland to the pairtie, keparis and fulfillaris of thair pairt thairof or euir thay be hard in judgement thair failze and brek, being first knawn and kend and siclyke, the Clan makgillehaynich bindis and oblissis thame thair airis and successouris that thay, nor nane that they may stop or lat do hurt nor harme in ony tymes cuming in persoun or guddis to ony that dwellis within the Erll of Ergyllis cuntrie bot as law ordainis, under the paine foresaid and baith the saidis pairteis hes fund the personis underwrittin of thair propir confessionis soureteis and cautionaris for thame for fulfilling all and sindrie the premisses respective ilk ane thair awin pairt thairof and the saidis cautionaris Bindis and oblisses thame thair airis and assigneis in the said cautionarie and baith the saidiss pairteis bindis and oblisses thame

thair airis and assigneis to relief and skaithles keip
thair said cautionaris of the said cautionarie:
Cautionaris for the said Clan makillehaynych.
Donald Campbell of Duntrone, Cautioner for twa
    hundreth and fyftie merkis,
Mr Neill Campbell, Bishop of Argyll [1580-1608],
    Cautioner for twa hundreth and fyftie merkis, and
John dow me.allane vc.sorle of Shwnay, Cautioner for
    fyve hundreths merkis.
And Hector Maklane of Doward to releif the saidis
    Cautioneris according to his oblissing.

(Here follows the usual clause of registration in the
Sheriff Court Books of Argyll.)

IN WITNESS HEIROF baith the saidis pairteis and
Cautionaris hes subscriwit thir presenits as followis
zeir, day and place foresaid
Befoir thir witnessis,
Archibald Campbell of Barbrek, creggenis,
Archd. Campbell of makgillespik vc.eane (or *baine*) in
    Kilmolrwe.
Donald rewaich makdonill (or *makdonchie*)
    makdunlaif in Ardlarach in Looing,
Johne makgillechallum, vc.ane vek donill,
Donald makgillechallum, his broder Officiar of
    Kreggenis,
Gillespik makgillecreist vc. Larty and
Gillespik makane gwrm vekdoull Creggenis.

(signed) Ronald Campbell of Barrichbeyan

Signed personally by Hector Makleane off Doward at Kilmartin, 24 June, 1604, before Duncan Campbell of Ulway, Archibald Campbell of Barbrek and Duncan M'Doneill V'Olchallum of Poltalloch.
Signed by John Dow of Shuna by James Kincaid, notary.
Signed personally by Donald Campbell off Duntrone.
Signed personally by Mr Johne Campbell, as cautioner, but 'onlie to the tyme that my father Mr Neill Campbell returne home godwilling nixt eftir this twentie fourth of Junij 1604 and thaireftir to be as frie as I was befoir the subscriptioun heirof.[17]

1614 proved the fateful year for the Clan, when Archibald Campbell, seventh earl of Argyll, having appointed Ronald Campbell of Barrichbeyan, bailie of Jura, conveyed to him on 19th July, 1614, the undernoted properties in south Jura, and Proaig, in Islay, formerly belonging to the Lords of the Isles, which had been previously conveyed to him with other areas of Argyll.[18]
Knockbraec,
Ardfin,
Strone,
Aschaleck,
Sonnaig,
Crackaig,
Kilearnadale,

---

[17] Campbell, *History of Craignish*, 277-280.
[18] *The Register of the Great Seal of Scotland,* 1593-1608, ed. J. M. Thomson, Edinburgh, 1890, 694-6.

Knockfeolaman,
Lergybreck,
Ardfernal,
Proaig,
Islands,
    Am Fraoch Eilean,
    Creig Island,
    Glass Island.[19]

The MacGilleChainnichs gave their support to the Macdonalds against the Campbells in a skirmish, at Knockrome, in Jura, which was now one of the properties of Ronald Campbell of Barrichbeyan. Among the Campbells, young John Campbell of Craignish pursued a group of MacDonalds which was under the leadership of Colkitto Gillespie MacDonald. In the ensuing fight, Dubhsith MacGilleChainnich of Lagg wounded John Campbell and Colkitto Gillespie killed him outright. Some forty men were killed in the affray.[20]

It is recorded that, 'in resentment of the slaughter of this John Dou, for so his brother was nicknamed, being black-hair'd, Ronald encounters a cluster of the MacGilleChainnichs, in 1614, whom he had been long looking for, and in revenge slew, in one morning, fifteen of them not sparing the chief of them, though at that time married to his own sister, viz. the proprietor of Mulbuie, who, it seems, by an expression, procured his own death; when he saw the rest of his friends slain, is

---

[19] Ibid. 609-20, 697-8.
[20] Youngson, *Jura*, 90-94.

said to have cried out, "Ronald, is not little John Dou['s] death sufficiently paid?" The other, being dipt in rage and blood, made answer with an oath, "If he is not, he shall be." And, with the word, lends one blow and finished him. His common weapon was a large two-handed sword still kept in the house of Craignish and his armour-bearer was John More, McNokaird, with whom I spoke being then in his old age past 90 and died in the year 1684.[21]

'A remission for this slaughter, under the Register of the Great Seal, lies in the house of Craignish. After this action, Ronald, either being afraid of his ill neighbours or feigning to be afraid, goes straight to [Archibald Campbell,] the [eighth] earl of Argyll, and told him that his house in Barrichbeyan was no way sufficient to screen him from the nocturnal attempts of his enemies upon him, and therefore entreated that he might allow him the house of Craignish to live and that he would prove as sufficient a chamberlain as the present one, who, at that time, happened to be Colin More Campbell … son to the former mentioned Archibald and the possession of the house … his posterity of it continued to this day … Campbell, Auchinbreck's son … whom he dispossessed, having got the Chamberlainry.'[22]

This slaughter broke the Clan in Jura. It scattered and ceased to exist, as such, as a high proportion of the men of the Clan were killed, which was a significant

---

[21] Campbell, *History of Craignish*, 243-4.
[22] Ibid.

part of the total population: only 100 fighting men are recorded as being in Jura and Scarba in 1593.[23]

---

[23] Sibbald MS. *West Highland Notes and Queries,* March, 1988, Series 2. No. 1. 8.

CHAPTER 6

Jura in the Eighteenth Century

The following document had the effect of reducing
members of the Clan to bonded tenants, at best, as Jura
and Islay became the property of others from the time
of their of tenure of their land on any of the estates after
that date. The clearances began in the middle of the
seventeenth century until almost the end of the
nineteenth century.[1] The resultant emigration is dealt
with by Youngson,[2] and a specific account has been
given of the emigrants in North Carolina.[3]

REGULATIONS FOR JURA TENANTS OF 1743
by Archibald Campbell of Jura.

MEMORANDUM OF WHAT THINGS ARE TO BE
PROCLAIMED TO THE TENANTS UPON SUNDAY
9TH MAY 1743

Imp: They are to sett the half of their Potatoes in old
land under the Penalty of five shillings sterling to each

---

[1] Eric Richards, *The Highland Clearances*. vol.1. *Agrarian
transformation and the evictions, 1746 to 1886,* London,
1982.

[2] Youngson, *Jura,* 270-325.

[3] *Argyll Colony Plus, Special edition, Journal of the North
Carolina Scottish Heritage Society*, Laurinburg, N.C., U.S.A.,
March, 1998, volume 12, No.1, a copy of which has been
lodged in the Library of the Scottish Genealogy Society,
Edinburgh.

Person that shall be guilty of a breach of this Act, being the Staint upon each two pence of Land within the whole Bailirie.

Itt. They are to divide the Wintertown whenever the Crop is gathered for the first and second year of their Tack, and each Tennant to cleanse his Proportion of the same, under the Penalty of a Crown upon each twopenny land if it is not done within the 2nd year.

Itt. They are yearly to divide their Heath and cleanse the same under the Penalty above-mentioned upon each two penny during their Tack.

Itt. Every town within the whole Bailirie is to keep two sufficient Bulls for their Catle after this year, during all the remaining years of their Tack, under the Penalty of Two Pound Sterling to each Town that shall be guilty of a breach of this Act.

Itt. They are all to goe regularly to the shielding under the Penalty of a Crown to each Person that shall stay for one day longer than the rest of the Neighbours.

Itt. They are all to cast their peats regularly as the Officer and any other two persons appointed by the Bailie shall direct them, under the Penalty of ten shillings sterling upon each 2 penny land.

Itt. They are not to keep or make use of any Schringeing Nets under the Penalty of five pound Sterling to each Person guilty.

Itt. Any person that is guilty of theft to the value of a sixpence is to lose his Tack and a fine imposed upon him according to his crime.

Itt. Any Person that is found guilty of bad Neighbourhiade is to lose the benefit of his Tack.

Itt. Any Person that shall putt any beaste unto any of the Isles without liberty is to pay a Crown for each beaste.
Itt. All the Towns below Ardmenish are to send eight Botles of straw to thatch the Miln and Smidy every two years during their Tack, and the Milner and Smith to thatch the same, and to send it to the Miln and Smidy before the eight Day of October.
Itt. Any Person that has Oversums is to put away the same before the first of June or to forfeit all the Oversums to the Master.
All the fines that shall be collected by any breaches of the things above mentioned to be equally divided between the Master and the poor of the Parish.[4]

There is little extant documentary evidence regarding the actual inhabitants of Jura under the frequent changes of tenancies, except from sheriff courts records.[5]

Warned of removal by Archibald Campbell of Jura.
2nd April, 1793.
Angus Shaw, Kille
Archibald Shaw, Kille
Donald Shaw, Brosdale
Duncan Shaw, Lussagiven
Argyll Sheriff Court Summons, NAS.SC.54/2/179.

---

[4] Youngson, *Jura*, 367-8.
[5] Scott Buie, *The People of the Parish of Jura, Scotland, 1500-1811*, Burlington, Texas, 2003. Recording the Argyll Sheriff Court Summonses.

Warned of removal by Donald MacNeill of Colonsay.
9th May, 1735.
Catherine Shaw, Ardlussa
Donald Shaw, elder, Ardlussa
Donald Shaw, Ardlussa
Donald Shaw, younger, Ardlussa
Duncan Shaw, Ardlussa
John Shaw, Ardlussa
Neil Shaw, Ardlussa
Argyll Sheriff Court Process SC54/2/47.

MacNeill appears to have occupied this property for some time before 11th January, 1737 when he purchased Ardlussa and Knockintavil[6] from John MacLean of Lochbuie.[7]

4th April, 1757.
Donald Shaw, senior. Knockintavil
Donald Shaw, junior, Knockintavil
Donald Shaw, tenant of the 'pendicle of Knockintavil called Carn'
Duncan Shaw, Knockintavil
Argyll Sheriff Court Process SC54/20/3/31.

4th April, 1760.
Hugh Shaw, of the 'pendicle of Knockintavil called Achadadine in Glengarrisdale'
Mary Shaw, Knockintavil
Argyll Sheriff Court Process SC54/2/84.

---

[6] Since the twentieth century the place, now with only one dwelling house, has been known as Barnhill.
[7] Youngson, op.cit., 391.

Warned of removal by Archibald MacNeill of Colonsay, succeeded, 1773.
4th April 1777.
Angus Shaw, Ardlussa
Donald Shaw, Ardlussa
John Shaw, An Carn
John Shaw, Knockintavill
Neil Shaw, Senior, Ardlussa
Neil Shaw, Junior, Ardlussa
Argyll Sheriff Court Process SC54/2/131.

18th March, 1791.
Allan Shaw, Ardlussa
Catherine Shaw, Lussagiven
John Shaw, Lealt
Neil Shaw, Ardlussa
Argyll Sheriff Court Process SC54/2/171.

Warned of removal by Archibald Campbell, fourth of Jura, succeeded, 1764.
2nd April, 1793, Summons, SC54/2 /179
Angus Shaw, Kille
Archibald Shaw, Kille
Donald Shaw, Brosdale
Duncan Shaw, Lussagiven
John Shaw, Kille
John Shaw, Lagg
John Shaw, Lussagiven
John Shaw, Craighouse and Changehouse, part of Drinitorran
Neil Shaw, Knockcrome

Neil Shaw, Lagg
Argyll Sheriff Court Process SC54/2/179.

4th April, 1794.
Malcolm Shaw, Knockintavill
Argyll Sheriff Court Process SC54/2/182.

Waves of emigrants commenced in 1767 and the population continued to fall over the decades. The population of Jura and Colonsay fell from 2205, in 1831, to 1342, fifty years later. The resident population is now some two hundred with only one resident Shaw.

CHAPTER 7

Scarba

Scarba, an island just north of Jura near the Gulf of Corryvreckan, is now uninhabited except when Kilmory Lodge is occupied during the shooting season while the building at Molbowie is used by campers as an outward bound centre, the site of the home of the last Chief of the Clan, when the island was owned by Hector MacLean, ygr. of Lochbuie, which his ancestors had held for centuries. The Chief lived at Mulbuie, later known as Molbowie, with his wife, a sister of Ronald Campbell of Barrichbeyan, who killed him.[1] He was probably buried in the graveyard of Cill Mhoire, which fell into disuse by the middle of the eighteenth century. Members of the Clan continued to live there long after the fall of the lordship of the Isles until the nineteenth century.

The following are recorded at Argyll Sheriff Court:

Summons issued on 27th February, 1779, against Neil Shaw, Mulbuy, Scarba, and others for payment of debt, including a matter of a boat, to Duncan Campbell of Glendarvell and John MacDougall.
Argyll Sheriff Court Process SC/54/2/135.

Warned of removal by John McDougall of Lunga, 25th February, 1783.
Archibald Shaw, Mulbuy

---

[1] Cf. supra p40.

Malcolm Shaw, Mulbuy, Scarba
Argyll Sheriff Court Process SC54/2/148.

14th January, 1785.
Malcolm Shaw, Kilmory, Scarba
Argyll Sheriff Court Process SC54/2/154.

24th February, 1786.
Donald Shaw, Kilmory, Scarba
Malcolm Shaw, Kilmory, Scarba
Argyll Sheriff Court Process SC54/2/157.

Warned of removal by John and Neil MacPhail,
Dunloskin, 4th April, 1787.
Neil Shaw, Mulbuy, Scarba
Argyll Sheriff Court Process SC54/2/160.

15th February, 1788.
Donald Shaw, Mulbuy, Scarba
Malcolm Shaw, Mulbuy, Scarba
Summons executed 25th February 1788, witnessed by
    John McLean and Angus McDougall of Kilmory.
Argyll Sheriff Court Process SC54/2/162.

CHAPTER 8

Islay

The original inhabitants of Islay were the Cenél nOengusa.[1] Thus there are only a few MacGilleChainnichs to be found there.

There are but two entries in the Exchequer Rolls. The first is Duncan MacGilleChainnich, a king's tenant in Islay 8th June, 1506, paying a rent of £5.9.[2] The other appears in the Tack and Rental of Islay, made at the castle of Dunyvaig, 5th July, 1541, by the lord commissioners before written to the persons following, their entry thereto to be at the feast of Whitsunday preceding the date hereof, viz., in anno 1541:

'The Midward of Islay: Carrapols, xxv s. land. Assedatur Neill McIllanich (MacGilleChainnich) pro spatio predieto, paying yearly iii marts (cow or ox) fattened, killed and salted and stored about Martinmas for winter use, iii wethers (male sheep) vii s. vi d. money xxii stone half stone cheese xxii stone half stone meal iii geese iii fowls.'[3]

In June, 1614, John Campbell of Cawder offered a rent of 8000 merks yearly and a grassum of £2000 for Islay, proposing, in general terms, methods of reducing

---

[1] Bannerman, *Dalriada*, 116.

[2] *Accounts of the Lord High Treasurer of Scotland*, edd. T. Dickson and J. Balfour Paul, Edinburgh, 1877-1916, xii., 709.

[3] *E.R.*, xvii., 617, 638.

the island.[4] James MacDonald offered a similar sum.[5] Cawder was prevailed upon to up the bidding, 'to consent to accept the feu of Islay upon conditions far above anything that any responsall man of quality did eve offer for it,' and persuaded to undertake an expedition at his own expense.[6]

When, on 11th October, 1615, he took possession of Islay. To secure support, he sealed bands with the tenants of Islay: the MacBrehons, the Mackays and the Maceacherns.[7]

In January, 1619, some twenty five representing the great Campbell branches and their allies met in Inverary and subscribed to a band.[8]

'Clanship and kinship were supremely important in this tempestuous period in highland history and the internal decline of the MacDonalds is a more satisfactory explanation of their downfall than theories of Campbell manipulation, although external interference was, undoubtedly, a factor. The Campbells, in contrast, by recognising the importance of and by acting to protect the bonds of kinship, prevented

---

[4] *Calendar of State Papers, Domestic, 1611-18,* ed. M. A. E. Green, London, 1871, 234.

[5] D. Gregory, *History of the Western Highlands and Isles of Scotland from 1493 to 1625,* Edinburgh, 1836, 359.

[6] Denmylne MSS in Highland *Papers,* ed. J.R.N. Macphail, Edinburgh, 1920, iii., 256.

[7] *Book of the Thanes of Cawdor,* ed. Cosmo Innes, Spalding Club, Aberdeen, 1859, 242.

[8] Ibid., 243-5.

The custody of this royal castle, with Cairnburgh and Iselborgh, with the lands and small islands appertaining to them, was given by David II in 1343 to John, Lord of the Isles. In 1390, Donald, Lord of the Isles, granted Lachlan MacLean of Duart various lands and castles, including half of the constabulary of the castle of Dun Chonaill, together with lands in and near the Garvellachs.

When Dun Chonaill passed to Archibald Campbell, seventh earl of Argyll, he directed the removal of the last MacGilleChainnich family, in January 1631. In all probability, they were the descendants of the first keepers appointed by the Lord of the Isles. He granted the property to Colin Campbell, minister of Craignish, and his son. Neil MacVicar, a messenger, was sent to Dun Chonaill castle, and ejected MacGilleChainnich, his wife, children and his tenants.[8]

As the castle and its precincts were small and only providing modest support for a few people, it is apparent that MacGilleChainnichs had occupied the island since at least the time of the Lordship. It is possible that they were there as priests from early times. There is still a cell extant on the small island of Cul-Bhreanain reputed to have been occupied by St Brendan.[9] More significant is the remains of a small monastery founded on Eileach a Naoimh by him.

---

[8] Argyle Transcripts, quoted in *The Clan Campbell*, ed. A. Campbell, Inverary, 1973, 191.

[9] G. A. Frank Knight, *Archaeological Light on the Early Christianizing of Scotland*, Edinburgh, 1933, 387.

Details are described[10] and an illustration of the chapel and beehive cells is given.[11] There are now no residents.

---

[10] Ibid., 387-8.
[11] Ibid., facing, 236.

CHAPTER 10

Eighteenth Century References to Macgillechainnich

The following appear in the old parish register of Rothesay:

Mary MacGilleChainnich, daughter of Dougal MacGilleChainnich and Ann Campbell, in the parish of Inverary and Glenarary, 10th June, 1722.

Duncan MacGilleChainnich or Shaw, distiller in Rothesay, son of Archibald MacGilleChainnich, in the Island of Islay, and Margaret Galbraith, daughter of Neil Galbraith in Kilmachmaig, m. 5th June, 1791.

Angus MacInnes, weaver in Rothesay, son of Colin MacInnes, in the parish of Bowmore, and Catherine MacGilleChainnich or Shaw, daughter of the deceased John MacGilleChainnich, in the parish of North Knapdale, m. 3rd December, 1793.

Neil MacGilleChainnich, weaver in Rothesay, son of John MacGilleChainnich, in the Island of Islay, and Janet Leitch, daughter of the deceased John Leitch, in the parish of Kilmun in Glassary, m. 19th December, 1794, son of Archibald, b. 12th November, 1797 registered with MacGilleChainnich surname.

Patrick McKinnon, seaman in Rothesay, son of Hugh McKinnon, in the Isle of Skye, and Janet MacGilleChainnich, daughter of the deceased John MacGilleChainnich, in the parish of North Knapdale, m. 9th November, 1797.

Robert MacGilleChainnich, son of William MacGilleChainnich or Shaw, and Janet Brown, in parish of Rothesay, b. 24th June, 1798.

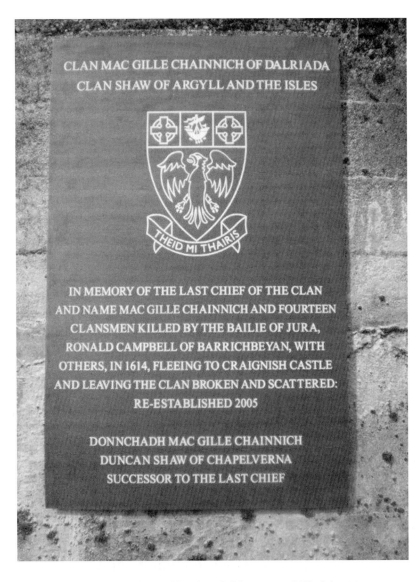

CLAN MAC GILLE CHAINNICH OF DALRIADA
CLAN SHAW OF ARGYLL AND THE ISLES

THEID MI THAIRIS

IN MEMORY OF THE LAST CHIEF OF THE CLAN
AND NAME MAC GILLE CHAINNICH AND FOURTEEN
CLANSMEN KILLED BY THE BAILIE OF JURA,
RONALD CAMPBELL OF BARRICHBEYAN, WITH
OTHERS, IN 1614, FLEEING TO CRAIGNISH CASTLE
AND LEAVING THE CLAN BROKEN AND SCATTERED:
RE-ESTABLISHED 2005

DONNCHADH MAC GILLE CHAINNICH
DUNCAN SHAW OF CHAPELVERNA
SUCCESSOR TO THE LAST CHIEF

Memorial to the Clan Chief and Clansmen killed in 1614
©David Rain

CHAPTER 11

The Clan Memorial at Kilearnadale Cemetery, Keils, Isle of Jura

On the right hand side of the entrance to the ancient cemetery of Kilearnadale, dedicated to St Ernan, as also is Chapelverna, there is a plaque in memory of the last Chief of the Clan and Name of MacGilleChainnich and his fourteen Clansmen who were killed in Jura by Ronald Campbell of Barrichbeyan, bailie of Jura, and his followers, in 1614.

The memorial was erected by Duncan Shaw of Chapelverna, recognised successor to the last Chief, as the Representer of the Clan and Name MacGilleChainnich of Dalriada, Shaw of Argyll and the Isles, on 14th May, 2005, by Robin O. Blair, Lord Lyon King of Arms.

It was unveiled on 27th August, 2011, by The Honourable Duncan Shaw, Vancouver, a descendant of a Jura family who emigrated to Canada in the mid-eighteenth century.

Three years later, on 9th August, 2014, a Clan gathering was held at Kilearnadale, on the four hundredth anniversary of the murder of the last Chief and his fourteen clansmen. During the act of remembrance, conducted by Mrs Angela Stather, a wreath was laid at the memorial by Miss Erika Ruth Shaw, the Representer's daughter, and Miss Selima Rain, a grandniece of The Honourable Duncan Shaw, read Ecclesiasticus, chapter 44.

Members of the Clan MacGilleChainnich in chronological order

d.a.1423 Dominic, rector of St Congar of Waternish, Duirinich
[NG2045]. *C.S.S.R.*, 1423-28, 203-4, 206.

a.1421 Donald, Premonstratensian canon, St Mary's Boyle
in the diocese of Elphin, Ireland. *Calendar of
Entries in the Papal Registers,* ed. J. A. Twemlow,
London, 1906, vii. 193, 1909, viii. 50.

1421- Duncan, abbot of Iona, [NM2723]. *The Heads of
d.1465 Religious Houses in Scotland from Twelfth to
Sixteenth Centuries,* edd. D.E.R. Watt and N.F.
Shead, Edinburgh, 2001, 112.

1427 Maurice, former parson of St Congar of Knoydart
[NG8301], patron Lord of the Isles. *C.S.S.R.,* ii.
180-1.

1456 Duncan, secretary to John Macdonald, earl of Ross
and Lord of the Isles, in *Acts of the Lords of the
Isles*, 1336-1493, edd. Jean Munro and R.W.
Munro, Edinburgh, 1986, 92, probably archdeacon

1461 of the Isles, 1461. *Fasti Ecclesiae Scoticanae
Medii Aevi Ad Annum 1628*, edd. D.E.R. Watt,
and A. L. Murray, Edinburgh, 2003, 273.

1506 Duncan, in Islay. *E.R.*, xii. 709.

1537 John, bailie of Wigtown, [NX4365], *E.R.*, xvii. 66,
burgess, 420, *E.R.,* xviii, 420.

1541 Neil, Carrapols, Islay. *E.R.,* xvii. 617, 638.
Ivoy, Lyel and Lephinstrath [Lephinmore, NR9892:
Lephinmorechapel, NR9590], *E.R.,* xvii. 632.
Donald MacGilleCallum, Pubil [NN4642], *E.R.,* xvii.
629.

1541 — MacGilleChainnich, Macriebeg [NR3249], *E.R.,*
xvii. 632.
1546 Malcolm, curate, Strathfillan [NN3428], Charters of
Campbell of Lawers.
Donald, murdered John MacClerich in Aberlour
[NJ2643], *Register of the Privy Seal of Scotland,*
1542-1548, edd. D. Hay Fleming and James
Beveridge, Edinburgh, 1936, iii. 2745.
1570 Duncan, vicar of Craignish [NM7701], *O.P.S.,* i. 96.
1580 Gillespie, Chapelverna. *Strachur Writs,* iv. 47-49.
1598 Ian Roy, Strachur [NN0901]. *Strachur Writs,* iv. 43,
Chapelverna, 1617, ibid., 47-49.
1599 Duncan O'Neil, stole from Malcolm McQueen of
Grantully, *Register of the Privy Council of*
Scotland, 1613-16, ed. David Masson, Edinburgh,
1891, vi. 489.
1604 Angus Macdonchie, Manuscript History of Craignish
by Alexander Campbell, Advocate, ed. Herbert
Campbell, Miscellany of the Scottish History
Society, Edinburgh, 1926, iv, 277-80.
Donald makangus, ibid.
Donald makeane vekconill, ibid.
Donald oig makdonill vekdowsey, ibid.
Duncan oig, nephew of the foregoing, ibid.
Duncan oig makangus, ibid.
Duncan oig makdonill vekconchie, ibid.
Gillecallum son of Donald oig makdonill
vekdownsey, ibid.
GilleCallum makangus, ibid.
Gillecreist makangus, ibid.
John oig makangus, ibid.
John dow makean vekdonill, ibid.
John makdonill vekconchie, ibid.
John ower makangus, ibid.
Neil makangus, ibid.

1604	Neil makdonill vekdonchie, ibid.
1615	Donald, Cairndow [NN1711]. MacPhail, *Strachur Writs,* iv. 46.
d. 1615	GilleChainnich, son of Donald, Craigdow [NN1711], ibid., iv. 46.
1632	Duncan, Strachur [NN0991], ibid., iv. 49.
	Iain McIlespic Vc Iain roy, Chapelverna, ibid., iv. 47-9.
1655	Effie, widow, Strachur [NN0991]. *The Minutes of the Synod of Argyll, 1652-1661,* Edinburgh, 1944, ed. Duncan. C. Mactavish, ii. 78.
1657	John, elder, at presbytery of Dunoon, ibid., ii. 161.
1660	John, Jura [NR5379], ibid., ii. 229-30.
	Archibald, servant of John Campbell of Carrick, descended from the Campbells of Ardkinglas, hereditary keeper of the castle [NS1994], admitted burgess, Inverary. *The Burgesses of Inverary,* 1665-1963, edd. Elizabeth A. MacIntyre and Sheila Beaton, Scottish Record Society, Edinburgh, 1998, 2.
1663	Patrick, of General Grant's Company, admitted burgess, Inveraray, 1663, ibid., 5.
1669	Gillecallum, Leackmore, NS0498, to be removed. McPhail. *Strachur Writs,* iv. 222.
	Neil, Ballachuan, Ballichoan in Seil [NM7617], to be removed, ibid., iv. 224.
1672-1693	Duncan, in the household of Anneta, eldest daughter of Archibald Campbell of Kilmun, wife and later widow of Colin Campbell of Strachur, after his death in 1685, whose heir, Alistair, never married and died c. 1697. Cameron, *Justiciary Records of Argyll and the Isles, 1664-1742,* 105, List.
1675	John, Inverneil, [NR8481], ibid., 50, 52.
1678	Archibald, Glenbranter [NS1097], ibid., 88.
	Archibald, Glensluan [NS0999], ibid., 88.

1678	Gilneive, Feorlin [NR5369], ibid., 98.
	John, Chapelverna, ibid., 97, m. Susanna, daug. of Archibald Gillespie of Ballimore, minister of Strachur and Strathlachlan, 1700-50. *Fasti Ecclesiae Scoticanae*, ed. Hew Scott, second edition, Edinburgh, 1923, iv., 45.
	John Moir, tailor, Cregganinver [NN0891]. Cameron, *Justiciary Records of Argyll and the Isles, 1664-1742*, 88.
1678, 1693	John Succothmore [NN1301], ibid., 88. List.
1678	Patrick, Dowfeorlin, 1678, ibid., 88.
1679	John ban, Gerfeorlin, ibid., 105.
	John, Leanach, NS0497, ibid., 100.
1680	Moir, wife of Archibald MacVicar of Stronemagachane. *Index to the Particular Register of Sasines for Argyll*, 636.
1685	Donald, Kilbride, Craignish, Duncan C. MacTavish, *The Commons of Argyll*, Lochgilphead, 1935, 9, 21.
	Donald, Glenshellich, NS1197, ibid., 16.
	Donald, Strachurmore [NN1201], ibid., 12.
	Duncan, Bellanoch [NR8092], ibid., 15.
	Duncan, Strachurbeg [NN0901], ibid., 12.
	Neil, Achitangan, Kilmodan, Glen Daruel [NR9985], ibid., 13.
1692	Donald, Cuillchurrellune Kilchrenean [NN0322], 1692, ibid., 31.
	Donald, Muckloch, Derremenoch and Strone [NS1980], ibid., 52.
	John, Nether Lorn [NN0834], ibid., 34.
	Malcolm, Lailt, Drumanrianich, Indincallich, Indenbeg, and Gartveans, ibid., 53.
1693	Archibald, Ardglen, Strachur [NN2702], List.
	John, Stronegartan [NS1980], List.

1693 Margaret, Strachurbeg [NN0901], m. John, List.
Donald, Gereforlan, List.
William, Gereforlan, List.

1698 Moir, Ellister, Rinns, Islay [NR2157], murdered
April. Cameron, *Justiciary Records of Argyll and
the Isles, 1664-1742,* 177-8.

1708 John, servitor to Donald Campbell of Clachan,
provost of Campbeltown, burgess of Inverary, *The
Burgesses of Inveraray 1665-1963,* edd. Elizabeth
A. MacIntyre and Sheila Beaton, Scottish Record
Society, Edinburgh, 8.

1711 Archibald, Leanach [NS0497]. Cameron, *Justiciary
Records of Argyll and the Isles, 1664-1742.* 270.
Donald (or Duncan), Strone in Strathlachlan
[NS0194], ibid., 261, 265-6, 268, 272.
An unnamed Clan member, servitor to Patrick
Campbell, ygr. of Barcaldine, NM9641, ibid., 259.

1716 Donald, Aros [NM5645], *Inhabitants of the Inner
Isles 1716, Morvern and Ardnamurchan,* ed.
Nicholas Maclean-Bristol, Scottish Record
Society, Edinburgh, 1998, 4.
Donald, Cameron [NM6025], ibid., 54.
Angus, Lochbuie Castle [NM6124], owned by
Murdoch MacLean of Lochbuie, 1702-d.a.1726,
ibid., 55.
Donald, Lochbuie Castle [NM6124], ibid., 55.
Donald, Scallastle [NM6938], ibid., 62.
Duncan, Ardnadrochet, [NM7332], ibid., 65.
Patrick, Kilmary [NM5270] Ardnamurchan, ibid.,
112.

1726 Donald MacGilleChainnich Vic Vane, Gearin,
Strachur Writs, ii., 321.

1727 Archibald, Savory, lately servitor to Duncan
Stewart, drover in Appin, *The Justiciary Records*

	of Argyll and the Isles, 1705-1747, ed. John Imrie, Edinburgh, 1969. ii., 391, 400-1.
1727	Duncan, was in Drumnine, now in Appin, ibid.
1730	Neil McDoyll Roy, servitor to Allan McLean of Garmony [NM6740], ibid., 436-7.
1750	John McIllespie Vc Ean Roy, Argyll, *Index to the Particular Register of Sasines for Argyll, Dumbarton, Arran & Tarbert, 1617-1780,* Edinburgh, 1926, 636.
1750, c.1770	John, Chapelverna. Argyll Sasines, vol. 8. fol. 116, *A Directory of Landownership in Scotland,* ed. Loretta R. Timperley, Scottish Record Society, Edinburgh, 1976, 44.
1791	Duncan, distiller, Rothesay, [NS0864], son of Archibald MacGilleChainnich, in Islay, Marriage Register, Rothesay.
1795	Neil, weaver, Rothesay, [NS0864], son of John MacGilleChainnich, in Islay, ibid.
1797	John, in the parish of North Knapdale, d.a. Dec., 1797, ibid.
	William, son of Robert MacGilleChainnich, b. Kiltarlity, [NH5041], Birth Register, Rothesay.
b. Nov. 1797	Neil, Rothesay, [NS0864], son of Archibald Mac-GilleChainnich, Birth Register, Rothesay.
1822	John, Chapelverna. Disposition held by the writer.

Scottish Shaw lairds

Scottish Shaw lairds prior to 1700 recorded in The Register of the Privy Council or Register of the Great Seal of Scotland:

of Auchingairn, NS6169
of Bargarran, NS 4571*
of Barnhill [Bay NT1884]
of Broich, NN8620
of Cambusmore [Tower NS7792]
of Craigniebay [Knowe NX1873]

of Dalton, NY1174
of Dalwyne, NX3296
of Ditton, NS4034
of Dryholme, NY1251
of Duncanrig, NY0896
of Fordell [House NT1688]
of Fordhouse, NS2090
of Foulseils, NY4991
of Gartcarran, NS6685
of Glenmuir, NS5921
of Goldring, [Ayrshire]

of Grantully, NN 9152
of Greenock, NS2776*
of Grimmet, NS3210
of Haylie [Reservoir NS2158]
of Henryston, NS5625
of Kelsoland, [Kelso, NT7233]
of Kerse, NS8141
of Kilbride [Castle, NN7503]
of Knockhill, NT0693
of Lathangie, Kinross
of Pitmurthly, NO0820
of Polkemmet, NS9265
of Quilts, NO0211
of Sauchie [Tower NS8995]*
of Seggie, NO4419
of Sornbeg [Castle NS525]*
of Tillicoultry [NS9197]*

*Armigerous, recorded in Alexander Nisbet, *A System of Heraldry,* Edinburgh, 1722.